GW00468360

Volume Two

ex libris

Candlestick Press

Published by:
Candlestick Press,
Diversity House, 72 Nottingham Road, Arnold, Nottingham NG5 6LF
www.candlestickpress.co.uk

Design and typesetting by Craig Twigg

Printed by Bayliss Printing Company Ltd of Worksop, UK

Cover illustration © Marina Grau/Shutterstock

Candlestick Press monogram © Barbara Shaw, 2008

© Candlestick Press, 2023

Donation to Place2Be
www.place2be.org.uk

ISBN 978 1 913627 30 0

Acknowledgements

Thanks are due to the authors listed below for kind permission to use their poems,
all of which are published here for the first time:

Jane Burn, Jennifer Clark, Michelle Diaz, Louise Greig, HM Truscott,
Chitra Kalyani, Paul McDonald, Phoebe Robertshaw, Ali Rowland and
Frances Thompson.

Contents

		Page
Kindnesses	*Ali Rowland*	*5*
A Kindness of Ravens	*Louise Greig*	*6*
Imagine the first kind person	*HM Truscott*	*7*
In the loud cafe, next to the cabinet of cakes	*Michelle Diaz*	*8*
Brackets	*Chitra Kalyani*	*9*
A Nod To Saint Nicholas	*Jennifer Clark*	*10*
Be Kind to Pigeons	*Paul McDonald*	*11*
Nature Remembers the Lamb	*Jane Burn*	*12*
The Garden of the Heart	*Phoebe Robertshaw*	*13*
KINDNESS	*Frances Thompson*	*14*
Afterword	*Suzy Ensom*	*16*

Kindnesses

Throw some kindness up into the wind
and watch it flutter down like softening rain,
brushing against your skin and others' too.
Choose to shrug them off or let them in,
those pieces floating weightless as leaves,
tiny, barely there.

What type of kind would you like to feel?
Words, a blown kiss, the touch of a hand.

Watch them, they fight some strong opponents,
but they are still there, those little pieces,
filling the air.

Ali Rowland

A Kindness of Ravens

A goose for a traveller
A woodpecker for a carpenter
A gull for a sailor
A starling for a dreamer
A parrot for the lonely
A swallow for an acrobat
A blackbird for a piano tuner
A lark for a chorister

A kindness of ravens for
Samuel Taylor Coleridge
whose albatross taught us all;
He prayeth best who loveth best
All things both great and small

Louise Greig

Imagine the first kind person

No – imagine the first kind act.
Some Neanderthal kindness –
a cave, a fire, a hand stretched out.

See how we chip, chip, chip and shape
kindness; how it is our only tool –
hard and primitive and all we need.

(The huge sky and travelling clouds see nothing else.)

How we do not repay, but we turn round
and give again, on, into the dark
until our kindness is the shadow on the wall
of the living room, by lamplight.

HM Truscott

In the loud cafe, next to the cabinet of cakes

the ancient man with the quiet suit and liver spots
fell to the ground and my friend grew fast wings
and flew like a nurse-bird to his broken head.
She cupped his face and dabbed the blood,
then wiped the clots with a tiny *Kleenex*
from her pocket and carefully typed
numbers into her phone. She did not know him.
I stood back, yellow-bellied.
I squirmed at the sight of red. Nearly fainted.
She never flinched. Like a medic.
Like a mother. Her small bravery
put me to shame, showed me
that for all my pretty words about love, kindness is
an in the moment, selfless movement.

Michelle Diaz

Brackets

Mr. Ellis taught me French in high school.
He would not cross out your mistakes.
He would put them in brackets,
and write something above,
like a polite suggestion.

Years later you long for such kindness:
An arm from your left
An arm from your right
Holding you in a bracket
Asking you not to throw away your mistakes.

Chitra Kalyani

A Nod To Saint Nicholas

Like the French nuns who were inspired by you,
let us rise from warm beds and slip fruit
and justice into stockings, placing them
on the doorsteps of those who hunger.
On our last good night in this world,
whether dashing away by door or chimney,
may we, like you, leave a generous trail, thick
with kindness and stirring hope.

Jennifer Clark

Be Kind to Pigeons

Cherish any chance you get to hold a pigeon.
Its weight is just the space between your
palms, the message of a dream.

Be kind, and respect its expectations -
it flew through clouds of jewels to you,
powdered sapphire blue, mists of rubies.

Every feather fits. Admire its finery,
a history of pigeons printed in its plumage;
trust its whispered promise: one day you'll also fly.

Paul McDonald

Nature Remembers the Lamb

When your little life began, I opened up the sky —
filled it blue and flew each flag of bird especially
for you. I spread this lea, sweet beneath your feet
when I sensed your need for fields, when I heard
your tongue cry out for green. When you shivered
I sent these boughs to break the storm — When
your heart craved trees, each hand I owned became
a leaf. I learned your thirst and puddled my rain,
skimmed stars across the dark's pool to ease your fear —
wrote the moon above you. Turned the Earth, brought
you bright new days. Did you ever think that snow
could be so beautiful? I almost made it the colour
of you. The flowers beneath will be my gift. Whatever
you have needed it has been my pleasure to give.

Jane Burn

The Garden of the Heart

A kind heart is a garden
Flourishing with vitality
Carefully sowed with the seeds of benevolence,
Every compliment given
Every door held open
Every stranger smiled at
Spouts as a wand of tight green bud
From the depths of your soul,
Though as the weather patterns in nature
Our emotions can ebb and flow
Casting a hateful darkness over the budding verdancy
Extinguishing the benign flame cultivating the garden of your heart,
Yet the supple seedlings never wither
For a soul can be kind and imperfect
But never perfect and unkind.

Phoebe Robertshaw

KINDNESS

K. is for kind, as you are to me,
I. is for ideal, the perfect friend for me,
N. is for nice, always thoughtful & caring,
D. is for dedicated, generous & sharing,
N. is for nourishing & always being helpful,
E. is for encouraging words for which i'm very grateful,
S. is for sympathetic, trusting & good,
S. is for sweet, thank you for making me feel understood.

Frances Thompson

Afterword

Imagine the first kind person.

No - imagine the first kind act.

Now, imagine the first kind word. It's very special to see this volume of glorious poems of kindness take flight out into the world. It's no coincidence that many of the poems contain images of birds; kindness can be as light as a feather or a flutter of paper, but it is always a moving thing, travelling from one hand, one gesture, one person, to another. We all understand what kindness is, and means, but it can be both very simple and very complex, and these poems truly capture the infinite ways that kindness can be expressed. These poems are about kindness, but they also *show* kindness.

At Fair Saturday, we believe that there are two essential ingredients to building a better world: culture and social empathy. Our Kindness of Words programme celebrates the power of words and stories to bring people together and encourages people and communities to reach out to each other with kindness. We have been delighted to work with Candlestick Press over the past few years; poetry is an offering from poet to reader, and by sending these pamphlets instead of a card, this sharing ripples onwards and outwards. In a world which feels increasingly fragmented and frightening, these poems remind us that kindness may be weightless, but is powerful enough to fight strong opponents, and every tiny word or act of kindness brings light and hope. Holding open a door or smiling at a stranger can be an act of defiance against the chaos and unkindness that can sometimes feel overwhelming.

Each one of these poems is a gift of kindness, and it is our wish that these words will travel with you as a companion through your day, bringing whatever you need in the moment.

Suzy Ensom
Fair Saturday Foundation